SUPER UNDONE BLUE

ALSO BY SARAH ANNE COX

Arrival, Krupskaya 2002
Parcel, O Books 2006

SUPER UNDONE BLUE

Poems have appeared in the following publications:

Tangents, Dusie Kollektiv, Litmus Magazine and *11/11*.
The author thanks the editors of these publications.

Cover art: Sarah Anne Cox

Layout and Book Design: DUSIE
dusie.org | Kingston, RI

First printing, Sarah Anne Cox, 2016

ISBN: 978-1-944253-00-4

Library of Congress Control Number:
2015960904

CONTENTS

OF ORACLE BOATS AND GHOST SHIPS

LOCUST WOMEN

POLYXENA ERASURE &C.

OF ORACLE BOATS
AND GHOST
SHIPS

RE: HOPE

(for Pussy Riot)

My mother used to say
no, I will not calm down
rinsing the roots of a coconut palm
here, frost divides the pine needles
and snowflakes aren't special
just unrelenting
a case of conviction
sewing camp
red vestigial machines
line in sewn
       in mouths
Not even
the smudged glass
centuries of appeal
to the painted lady
hot breath whispered
etched in silver
the court room box
can escape iconography

HEREDITAMENT

The birds have been washed of tar oil
dishwashing liquid rinsed clean
no taint
the nested hatchlings chirp a bitter song
no yellow-feathered birds left
consanguineous
clothes horse
secret illness borne to bear
arousal hedgerow
a tiny blood stain
the manifold of disease
a beggars' almanac
in the ship's window
a flea and louse
a tripod burns whale oil
then sugar
then sexual appetite

OF ORACLE BOATS AND GHOST SHIPS

Relinquish to the sea what is owed
the summer wind brought down the Prada boat
little jumpers swarming and the speed
boats like mosquitoes
the massive black floating sideways leaking
enormous million dollar parts
into the bay the carbon tiller
the ragged red sail a zigzag
hoisted up, towed to dock

The grasses, brown
irrigation trench not dry but brackish from the burn
bent under the tremendous prow
the weight barely noticeable

Tend garden or island tend ship
or household what whispers through the fog horn
the fledgling Common Murres call out the names of
dead in passing
the center spot milky and calm
an upwelling of the sea floor

did you hear your name? someone elses?
Did they call you home as they
dove under? as they flapped up against the sea wind

There is no home for the sea bound
and this center section the respite
what remains dangerous and deep under,
farther even than the Cormorants can dive
the final resting spot, the reliquary
lest one washes onto shore picked at by gulls
Enormous pleasure craft bought for a song
in the recession, twin riches taking cover
in the wind shadow of Alcatraz
silver Prada helmets
and Swedish yellow to do one's bidding
have you a chariot in the race?
a goddess or an airline your patron

The corporate chantries for Emirates and Oracle,
for Vuitton and Prada
we have not come so far
beyond the reach of the servitude
beyond the blues and greens of nova Roma

The Terns screech from the old coast guard
station abandoned to tiny nests and the white
feathered make forays to the shore break

witness to the smoke flares off the bridge
the summer's wealth is not enough, the flag barren
and stark and the wind makes lonely council

LOCUST WOMEN

LOCUST WOMEN
Notes on Margaret Macdonald Mackintosh

THE MAY QUEEN 1900

Newcastle under Lyme
how the great white chalk
chronic landscape constructs
the body
Iterations and then again your little white dress
strewn
we are the locust women for the adjoining circle
rising from the earth
breast body breast hair do
the barely moving cocoons
angular head gear
anemic and treacherous
we have clotted
the groaning turned celestial
we have worn this weight of breast
on our backs

THREE PERFUMES, 1912

I have stopped breathing,
seriously only a wisp of me
puffy eyes
god made me into patterns and I absolutely stopped
but then she whispered in my ear
a pink smoke and I began singing
softly just barely audible in dog range
my design is the shoulder's fall and droop
my design is distance
I am in stasis because my nipples are my dress
if I could break free as the ladies next to me
my bow mouth breathes loss
like the two of swords
the reason I have stopped is the reason
but the pink smoke will catch me
always three sisters.

THE MYSTERIOUS GARDEN, 1911

The swell of my own making
so many wall flowers dressed
in blue tie
and shattered I am the wall so much
that I am the wall
I have swallowed myself in birthing and am
utterly alone
when I close my eyes there is no one there
or
I have dreamed of this moment
my singularity
for centuries
a song, a closed ring
I, a veritable gourd
not full but
like an egg sack that
rolls up with the wave
still intact
seeming fragile
though it has crashed in shore break

CINDERELLA 1901-23

Neither of us have feet
floating on vellum in this
puffed out air bag
There are more than our own hands here
others hold stake on my chest and
the pearls circling me,
the moment of someone else's magic

a salt wafer with frail hands
touching the rose's stub
she's been verbed
a casket of gestures in the various
hoops of the night and the skirt
This is the best thing that could happen.

SUPER UNDONE BLUE

After New York of 100 hotdogs
and 100 sprinks
natural history and water balloons and poses with
copied Easter island heads
or "We took this from them."
like the Met
searching for the "Wedding of Mary Cox"
her dress folded and put away now
the problem with transmissions
surging, huffing and pizza slice
and another hotdog, please.

We moor in Greece tied up five times and untied

The boy jumping from tall rocks
festooned
climate blued and greened
habilitated
plastic water bottle mythic
Orestes in his lawn chair
poking sand with his toes
meeting at a play date
7:PM Heracles
friends call him *Herk*
skinny and sinking under
while swimming
all these boy heroes
and Paris among them
jumping at his first fish
caught around cave-like, cove-like

Cigarette package
a circle with a line though it
slow eyed the most pointiest
part of the boat, stand there
secret nightlife of sea urchins
on the flat sand Mary steps on three

Limani, port
long pavement, gauntlet
super undone blue

Pork chops from the Minotaur
heroin and homemaking on the
other side of the electronic teller
downtown Athens
a new immigrant passage
Geiger counter
Chinese lantern signal land
filled with volcanic holes
black shadow
black urchin
black hole
black little old lady's dress

The problem with walking on a pebble beach
hobbled bare foot
not being able to pick and choose
the wet ones shine fantastic until they
dry and become plain again
when we've landed and churned up
making jewels and the fluff of clouds
the mermaid in her orange flippers can swim a blue
streak
but the road
the hill path from the cove, the walk to *gyros me pita*
calls for horse and carriage

What was wrong with ancient sailors?
there is no wine dark sea
no wine only the blue crystal oxygen twist
full fathom seen the little stones and urchins
and your continuous blue, your vacuous blue
hunting crosses for January's Halcyon
Theseus has become Christian and
Herakles has a summerhouse on Pelion

We've called for confusion, for
binding the edge to everyday clothes to
blinding counterfeit *Prada* hand bags
metal branding sun flash
the furies have chased you down the close
arteries of Plaka
with the memory of a flower
necklace and a double axe

This being the only place where you
might meet another girl named Phaedra you
might meet her here underneath the encaustic
canvas, here selling plastic Luna Park
chips having no where else to go
stuck in summer's stony beach threat
heaven filled with mosquitoes handy parasol sales
at intersection sides of a coin

Transcending the appendix
we are nothing but lists left in arrangements
of these repeating blues cleanly protesting the Greek
horizon does not get lighter but darker
with the abandoned cities the
hill forts Paris scaling the Knights of St. John
walls tipping the edges of the Sounion cape
exonerated from ruling foam calling smashed
against the cliff

POLYXENA ERASURE &C.

MEDEA 1-X

1

Iasonos, scribbled red in the eye
sojourn, that unending sea boat, ride sick
the death of children
murder , suicide , mercy
the mourning started long before that
churning flee
pieces of brother
what is jettisoned
from the ship
from the conscience
or before in a grove
secret vestige "old ways"
oath making is oath breaking
history's wreckage
doom was already
mountainous travels
not that ship again
sojourn and finally
this page pronouncing failure
jettisoned

2

Bronze mirrored girl
poor flower
crocus offered
sweetness *Glauke*
sweetings princess
but no stepmother likes
his children.
not gazing
banish murder

3

When it rained on the ship we huddled
under tented hides
wet fleece soaking through
later the sun would dry us out brittle
cracked earth, cauldron
the cup rolled from side to side with the sway, empty
head over the side
could see forever to the bottom
see our own wreckage resting
down there
couldn't dive deep enough to touch it
always floating just below the surface
that's how fate survived unchanged

4

Until now couldn't
reach my own doom
claimed
resurrected
killed
in a box is the terror
that will undo you
keep it closed Pandora and do not look
pass into darkness
my box open

5

Who gives up kingdoms?
even after feats of magic and awe striking deeds
oath breakers shake the pillars
deceit breeds deceit
two daughters cut up their father
and drop him into a pot
a mercy killing
the children bloodied yet whole
fly off to other plots their names
their poisons unknown
expatiation equation
yielding 40 days,
300 days, in exile
for x and y axis plotted
they sing here on the turn of the year
at one time they were innocent

6

The sea air makes even the dry seem wet
grains between the fingers melt
left bitter salt
and cork screw hair
we jettison the we for the I
When I came here from Iolkos, he says
as a stateless exile, thwarted. et cetera
I see myself in him
stateless and
ruined
the wretched who pull themselves
up on the backs of friends

7

Killer of brother king child
each claiming mere jealousy
an empty bed
a tiresome bed
the creak of old bones
we have not moved from this spot.

8

Beginning with sea trip
fantastic lark and times when he would
break down and weep for himself
his statelessness, his curse, his lucky sandal damned
by Hera loved by Chiron
Pelion Wood

9

In the scheme
he wavers handsome and despised
it was already decided
no returns no give backs
a bit of dirt on his shining skin
weary
paralyzed
we watch the scene unfold

10

To be lucky in life you must give
in slide into the frame with the
others a few hapless mistakes cannot ruin you
a few hapless mistakes can ruin you

11

Let yourself slide into the lines, slip in
unnoticed and live there in the dirt and
coarse gravel beach once we stepped off
the boat it was difficult to get back on
we did see the ships coming, laden
we lived among wealth and so the items arrived
for trade. sometimes I'd walk to the beach where
the ships pulled up to see if I was there, some part
of me, some eastern black sea part but all those
red faced men dissemble calling themselves from
no where. from the future.

12

To get to the beginning you must go backward.
You must file an affidavit of intent
You must pull up the claims in newspaper reports
You must listen patiently to every version
You must be prepared to argue anything.
You must stop cradling the baby and let him go
You must stop cradling the baby and murder

13

Embark
sea fairies surround us,
little twinkles of sea reflected
that evening we saw dolphins
who wanted to eat them
diving toward the prow
as if they would knock it off
but it hadn't rotted yet

14

I would never walk as far as the old Argo
it stank with survival
(shshshsh the eumenides
there rested in wait for me)
Where did you live?
on that boat.
Was that living?
no it was holding fast
to the mast.

15

It's a shame just to leave it there the pealing red paint
on her lip,
now silent and stateless but we hated it
everything it stood for
the cracked bench that could pinch the skin
the day when we washed regret off the deck
did I say regret, I meant blood

16

Climbing while sliding backward
the old trail covered with tiny pointed stones
slipping backward
dry dusted mouth
cracked lips

I am tripartite
normal, good, or bad
focus in and out on the sword
zoom to my goodness, helper maiden
obedient

17

We arrange our hands in a manner fitting
the station, the requirement of the moment
We arrange our hands so as to kiss other hands
if you have begged, just once, then
you know me, the angle of my dress folds,
wrung, the state of my diversion

18

Do you think I'm apologizing?
I'm not. There on the hillside coming down the pat
my son I have other worries, there is no water here
your hillside bandits don't scare me nor your king i
Troezen
by my hand fashioned
all of this.

19

Four Medeas
to the North death by hanging
to the farthest South a pipe
to the East and West the blade
we have remade ourselves in the new world.
over and over
each time a new twist, a little more distance
we are a little colder
more tired
more bound.

20

How shall we discuss this.
The spring chamomile oppresses
the senses and leaves me weak we
trek through the buzzing stumbling over stones
cast in the path someone's goats
have eaten all the
apples and left only the scent.

21

(for Kate Colby)
"And that is no small hurt for a woman?"

what did I mean by that
I meant Scottish luxuries
I meant you think we don't live by the sword
I meant you are rich and I am poor
I meant they will not laugh at me
I meant precarious rope tow
I meant snapped cord
I meant the wheat and the chaff
I meant you think you know a woman
I meant his bed was my bed
I meant that ancient tongue. Did he forget it?
I meant that ancient oath
I meant that bed is the same as social position
I meant I was worried about my bed.

22

The handbook of lies
I meant jealousy
telotupia
the tome of the vow
hand maiden to envy
here the table is cleared.
trapeza for the dead

23

Solvency
a raft kept us afloat.
we called that a boat
but it wasn't and he was the first to recognize it
on landing
so full of our journey
still glitter fell off us, our hands, our tongues
at dinner parties until it was
worn away.
we realized we were brassy
a dull glow

24

True story:______

25

It will pull you back. Pull you into your fate
hang the expense it is
honor and honor and honor
I do not mind so much dying.
I have placed my head above my
body.

26

I have horrified those who once loved me- even you have backed away
have backed away
those who at first rooted for me, saw me through
brought me the broth of consolation
I forgive the ladies, that they are shaken

27

It's true, I cried
wept so loud surprised myself
in coughs not moans
then I stopped
you will not get the best of me
I'm no cipher

28

Agamemnon was a dick
I didn't know him but I've heard

29

Pipe knife sword rope
thusly I kill my children
thusly I bind the ladies to me
thusly I kiss the hand
surrender to womanly gestures

30

There is no release in architecture
all those walls teaming
your stone on stone tumbled
in a single desperate request
for my children
it's too late
the boat prow has retrieved you
the lost ending of fostered home

31

My revenge was his revenge
Zeus, double edged
caught me in catching
the bird singer
the tongue removed
the body piecemeal

kin murder
kin rape
kin lineage
all of our crimes upon us

THE HIPPOLYTUS INFRACTION

From underneath some women take
a place steal a place
from under the wedge a perverse
shock giving rise to hand gestures that might prevent
evil
a spitting to the left and right
to return the bee women

PHAEDRA

Illness
I have made myself sick with it
inconvenient and unrequired
I rise only to revolt myself with
my own prurience
You glide by with your song and flower wreath
not a care

ALTARS AND SUBALTERNS

a garland for Artemis
From virgin meadow from virgin greenery
Hippolytus places reverent
from his pure soul
As much as he hates Aphrodite, she hates him
as much
her altar bare
but scripting death
the lopsided stage
as much as children make one
impure
the night's labors
her catastrophe a secondary consideration

URBAN CONSOLATION

two sided
if it is true that the childless make the
best midwives
then Artemis protects the entrance to the birth cave
the death pallet
ripe with rot
a song of the bright white daylight
she whispers,
if only lush meadows
a Thracian spear
not city walls, palace walls
not fountain
a defrocked head is madness
the pebbles and olives from a Cretan wood
inside lies illness
outside lies madness
Nurse, hide my head again

THESEUS

Gone to Apollo's faraway business
exiled and expatiated
for that mistaken black sail
for the Cretan daughters
scattered Aegean
to the sickly marriage bed
He is older now
his garlands freshly contrast
adventure in hand with disaster
a Troezen treason
the house shrieks to him
he cannot guess who
then cannot guess why
frozen by suffering
or by some event?

THE LABYRINTH

Phaedra said, The labyrinth is horrible.
It tricks you, thinking that you're going somewhere
Then it eats you, just like that.
A terrifying children's tale
Millennia later
What winds around
the work for god. What winds string
or thread of betrayal
of the dismissed
The clumsy broad stroke of Theseus'
will crushing fruit beneath his feet
sending a death wish on the cape of Nisiza
or abandoned to stars on Naxos
Better there than the ship
with black sails, dumb shrouds
clubs with thorns, what heroes lack is
the lacy edge of the Minotaur his
intricate pattern

BEE WOMAN

The bee consorts with the flowers to
contrive her yellow honey
her Cretan erotic history
the chastity of matrons
the taking of the honey for their own work
unfettered by desire
the bee woman makes
the quality of excess Pandora's
fascination
clotted waste
a bed produces attrition
the binary pornographic gaze
yet the bee women move on

NAXOS

Already born into sexual construction
Pasiphae, the bull dance
a thread pulled out of the darkness
her optional fever, descent
seven miles along the shore of Naxos
the piney forest hiding the sisters
who left on their own accord
who were brought, discarded
how to become a star of a story
when one is inconsequential

The standard of modesty
under things in the breeze
prayer and loathing lie beneath
the over pruned fig tree
not an accident of the body
the sack of which
the body's boundary of contents
he an empty vessel a hollow instrument
she a sack of chips and clots

PROVENANCE AND MANUSCRIPTS

She owns the sense of what it means not to be him
Bound inextricably to these walls
dark and wet with breath
coverings of veils and chants
She owns it but not the text
she owns the outsides of the words
both jagged and round vowels
the sharp serifs belong elsewhere

Surmising the abundance of verbs
we looked for her on the sides of buildings, the
symbol of a stone mason's
double axe under
then under and facing sideways
the inconsequential still leave a mark

POLYXENA ERASURE &C.

(From E's Hecuba Lines 345-3

I see you

touch your beard.

heart

I will

I must

my wish to die

unwilling

show

faint

should I

the Phrygians, be a bride keen

among suitors

over each

a goddess,

save for death name

long for

sounds savage

 buy me

make me

knead him

sweep his misery

while taint deemed royalty.

Lead me

see nothing

join in shameful treatment

whoever is not

yet neck
be dead
bereft
toil

LINE 195

ill boding rumor
of the wicked truth

Truth is wicked
the shore transforms
the dead speak
all over the dead can speak
Men in their brutish avenging demands
in the village, at the tomb, by the shore
come walk into the tent
the place of *Dike*, a tomb

DRESS MATTER

carnal dress peplos of the maid
carnal dress sexual pinning
the open sides of the peplos
the daughter's open dress
the pin missing

un done

Sarah Anne Cox is the author of *Arrival*, Krup-saya 2002 and *Parcel*, O Books 2006. Her work has appeared in the American anthologies *Bay Poetics* and *Technologies of Measure*. In 2014, her poems were translated into the Swedish. She lives in San Francisco where she teaches, wind-surfs, snowboards, and cares for her two children.

SIE
DU

9 781944 253004